CVS
Pocket Reference

Gregor N. Purdy

Beijing • Cambridge • Farnham • Köln • Paris • Sebastopol • Taipei • Tokyo

CVS Pocket Reference

by Gregor N. Purdy

Copyright © 2000 O'Reilly & Associates, Inc. All rights reserved.
Printed in the United States of America.

Published by O'Reilly & Associates, Inc., 101 Morris Street,
Sebastopol, CA 95472.

Editor: Chuck Toporek

Production Editor: Catherine Morris

Cover Designer: Hanna Dyer

Printing History:

> August 2000:   First Edition

Library of Congress CIP data is available at:
http://www.oreilly.com/catalog/cvspr/

ISBN: 0-596-00003-0   [1/01]
[C]

Table of Contents

CVS Pocket Reference

Introduction

The *CVS Pocket Reference* is a quick reference guide to the Concurrent Versions System (CVS). It describes the latest version available at the time of this writing, Version 1.10.8.

Conventions Used in This Book

The following typographic conventions are used in this book:

Constant width
> Indicates command-line computer output and code examples.

Constant width italic
> Indicates variables in examples. It also indicates variables or user-defined elements within italic text (such as pathname or filenames). For instance, in the path */usr/src/directory*, replace *directory* with a directory name.

Constant width bold
> Indicates user input in examples.

Italic
> Introduces new terms and indicates URLs, variables in text, user-defined files and directories, commands, file extensions, filenames, and directory names.

For More Information

The CVS home page is *http://www.cvshome.org.*

If you have the GNU `info` program installed on your system, you can type `info cvs` to view the online documentation. For some setups, this brings up the manual page in `info`, and for others, it brings up more information.

The same documentation is available in PostScript form as the paper "Version Management with CVS" by Per Cederqvist, et al. It can be found in the CVS distribution file */usr/local/src/cvs-1.10.8/doc/cvs.ps.* (Of course, you need to substitute a different directory name if you've installed the distribution somewhere other than */usr/local/src.*)

Also, basic information is available by running `man cvs` (on Unix-like systems). Running `cvs --help`, `cvs --help-options`, and `cvs --help-commands` provides still more information on the specified topics. To get help on a specific command, use `cvs -H` *command.*

Version Control and CVS

Version control (or *revision control*) is the practice of maintaining information about a project's evolution in order to retrieve prior versions of files, track changes, and (often most importantly) coordinate the efforts of a team of developers.

The *repository* (also called an *archive*) is the centralized area that stores the projects' files, managed by the version control system and the repository administrator. The repository contains information required to reconstruct previous versions of the files in a project. An administrator sets up and controls the repository using the procedures and commands described in the "Administrator Reference" section.

A *sandbox* (also called a *working directory*) contains copies of versions of files from the repository. New development occurs in sandboxes, and any number of sandboxes can be created from a single repository. Sandboxes are independent of each other and may contain files from different development stages of the same project. Users set up and control sandboxes using the procedures and commands found in the "User Reference" section.

In a typical interaction with the version control system, a developer checks out the most current code from the repository, makes changes, tests the results, and commits those changes back to the repository when they are deemed satisfactory.

Locking and merging

Some systems, such as RCS (Revision Control System) and SCCS (Source Code Control System), use a *locking model* that coordinates the efforts of multiple developers by serializing file modifications. Before making changes to a file, a developer must not only obtain a copy of it but must also request and obtain a lock on it from the system. This lock serves to prevent (really, dissuade) multiple developers from working on the same file at the same time. When the changes are committed, the developer unlocks the file, permitting other developers to gain access to it.

The locking model is pessimistic: it assumes that conflicts *must* be avoided. Serialization of file modifications through locks prevents conflicts. But it is cumbersome to have to lock files for editing when bug-hunting. Often, developers will circumvent the lock mechanism to keep working, which is an invitation to trouble.

Unlike RCS and SCCS, CVS uses a *merging model* that allows everyone to have access to the files at all times and supports concurrent development. The merging model is optimistic: it assumes that conflicts are uncommon and that when they do occur, it *usually* isn't difficult to resolve them.

CVS can operate under a locking model via the -L and -l options to the admin command. Also, CVS has special commands (edit and watch) for those who want additional development coordination support. CVS uses locks internally to prevent corruption when multiple people access the repository simultaneously, but this is different from the user-visible locks of the locking model previously discussed.

Conflicts and merging

In the event that two developers commit changes to the same version of a file, CVS automatically defers the commit of the second committer's file. The second developer then issues the cvs update command, which merges the first developer's changes into the local file. In many cases, the changes will be in different areas of the file, and the merge is successful. However, if both developers have made changes to the same area of the file, the second to commit has to resolve the conflict. This involves examining the problematic area(s) of the file and selecting among the multiple versions or making other changes that resolve the conflict.

CVS can detect only textual conflicts, but conflict resolution is concerned with keeping the project as a whole logically consistent. Therefore, conflict resolution sometimes involves changing files other than the one CVS complained about.

For example, if one developer adds a parameter to a function definition, it may be necessary to make all calls to that function pass an additional parameter. This is a logical conflict, so its detection and resolution is the job of the developers (with support from tools like compilers and debuggers). CVS doesn't notice this problem.

In any merge situation, whether or not there was a conflict, the second developer to commit often wants to retest the resulting version of the project, since it has changed since the original commit. Once it passes, the developer needs to recommit the file.

Tagging

CVS tracks file versions by revision number, which you can use to retrieve a particular revision from the repository. In addition, it is possible to create symbolic tags so that a group of files (or an entire project) can be referred to by a single identifier, even when the revision numbers of the files are not the same (which is often the case). This capability is often used to keep track of released versions or other important project milestones.

For example, the symbolic tag `hello-1_0` might refer to revision number 1.3 of *hello.c* and revision number 1.1 of *Makefile*. Symbolic tags are created with the `tag` and `rtag` commands.

Although the term *tag* is commonly used in the sense of *symbolic tag* (as created by the `cvs tag` command), Cederqvist, et al. use the terms *tag* and *revision* interchangeably. See the "For More Information" section for instructions on obtaining a copy of this paper.

Branching

The simplest form of development is *linear*, in which there is a succession of revisions to a file, each derived from the prior revision. Many projects can get by with a completely linear development process, but larger projects (as measured by the number of files, the number of developers, and/or the size of the user community) often run into maintenance issues that require additional capabilities. Sometimes it is desirable to do some speculative development while the main line of development continues uninterrupted. Other times, bugs in the currently released version must be fixed while work on the next version is already underway. In both of these cases, the solution is to create a *branch* (or *fork*) from an appropriate point in the development of the project. If, at a future point, some or all of the changes on the branch are needed on the main line of development (or elsewhere), they can be merged together (*joined*).

Branches are forked with the tag -b command; they are joined with the update -j command.

CVS Command Format

CVS commands take the form:

```
cvs global_options command command_options
```

For example, here is a simple sequence of commands showing both of these options in the context of creating a repository, importing existing files, and performing a few common operations on them:

```
$ cvs -d /usr/local/cvsrep init
$ cd ~/work/hello
$ cvs -d /usr/local/cvsrep import -m 'Import' ↵
  hello vendor start
$ cd ..
$ mv hello hello.bak
$ cvs -d /usr/local/cvsrep checkout hello
$ cd hello
$ vi hello
$ cvs commit -m 'Fixed a typo'
$ cvs tag hello-1_0
$ cvs remove -f Makefile
$ cvs commit -m 'Removed old Makefile'
$ cvs upd -r hello-1_0
$ cvs upd -A
```

Global options apply to both user and administrator commands, and other options apply only to one or the other. The common global options are described in the next section, and the user and administrator options are described in the "User Reference" section and the "Administrator Reference" section, respectively.

Common Global Options

Table 1 lists common global options that apply to both user and administrator commands.

Table 1: Common Global Options

Option	Description
-b bindir	Location of external RCS programs; this option is obsolete, having been deprecated at CVS versions above 1.9.18
-T tempdir	Absolute path for temporary files; overrides the setting of $TMPDIR
-v --version	Display version and copyright information

Gotchas

This section clarifies a few aspects of CVS that sometimes cause confusion:

CVS's file orientation
> While directories are supported, they are not versioned in the same way as traditional files. This is particularly important in the early stages of a project, when the structure may be in flux. Additionally, if the project is undergoing major changes, the structure is also likely to change. See the "Hacking the Repository" section.

CVS's text orientation
> There is no equivalent to diff for binary files, although CVS's support for binary files is usually sufficient. Use admin -kb to tell CVS a file is binary.

CVS's line orientation
> Moving a segment of code from one place in a file to another is seen as a delete (from the old location) and an unrelated add (to the new location).

CVS is not syntax-aware
> As far as CVS is concerned, small formatting changes are equivalent to sweeping logic changes in the same line ranges.

RCS anachronisms

CVS was originally built on top of RCS, but now all the RCS-related functionality is internal to CVS itself. RCS still shows up in the name of the $RCSBIN environment variable and the description of the -b option (both are now obsolete).

Installing CVS

This section describes the procedure for obtaining and installing the latest distribution of CVS. The instructions assume a Unix-like operating system. Typically, if CVS is going to be intalled for shared use, the procedures given are carried out as the root user.

Obtaining CVS

CVS releases that have one decimal point in their version numbers (such as 1.10) are the "stable" versions. Those with two decimal points (such as 1.10.8) are development releases. Generally, you should use the latest stable version, although development versions are in wide use and are quite stable too.

Some systems may already have an appropriate version of the CVS software installed. Check by issuing the cvs -v command. If cvs runs, it prints its version number; if it doesn't run, it may mean that CVS is not installed or that $PATH doesn't contain the appropriate directory. On many systems, running whereis cvs searches common installation locations regardless of the $PATH setting. If this doesn't turn up anything, try locate cvs to perform a broad search for files with "cvs" in their names. Not all systems support the locate command, so an alternative is to run find / -name cvs -print 2> /dev/null to look for any files named "cvs" on your system. This command searches every directory from the root directory, so it may take a long time to complete.

Only the source-based manual setup of CVS is described here, although some systems have special installation programs that allow you to download and install a binary package instead of downloading and compiling the source code yourself. Red Hat's RPM is one such package-management system.

Download the desired version of CVS from the main CVS FTP site (*ftp://ftp.cvshome.org*) or from one of its mirror sites (*ftp://ftp.cyclic.com/pub/MIRRORS*). The following example assumes CVS Version 1.10.8 is downloaded and compiled under */usr/local/src*:

```
# cd /usr/local/src
# ftp ftp.cvshome.org
Connected to ftp.cvshome.org.
220 ftp.cvshome.org FTP server
Name (ftp.cvshome.org:gregor): anonymous
331 Guest login ok, send your complete e-mail address as password.
Password:
230-ftp.cvshome.org
230-
230-NOTE: We've recently upgraded to the latest version of wu-ftpd.
230-This server more strictly adheres to the RFC protocols, and some
230-FTP clients work incorrectly.
230-
230-If you are not seeing directories, please try issuing an 'ls -l'
230-command as opposed to a standard 'ls' command.
230-
230 Guest login ok, access restrictions apply.
Remote system type is UNIX.
Using binary mode to transfer files.
ftp> cd pub/cvs-1.10.8
250-Please read the file README
250-it was last modified on Aug 16 16:13:31 2000 - 90 days ago
250 CWD command successful.
ftp> bin
200 Type set to I.
ftp> get cvs-1.10.8.tar.gz
local: cvs-1.10.8.tar.gz remote: cvs-1.10.8.tar.gz
227 Entering Passive Mode (208,184,89,16,42,5)
150 Opening BINARY mode data connection for cvs-1.10.8.tar.gz
    (2322238 bytes).
226 Transfer complete.
2322238 bytes received in 21.8 secs (1e+02 Kbytes/sec)
```

```
ftp> bye
221-You have transferred 2322238 bytes in 1 files.
221-Total traffic for this session was 2323233 bytes in 1 transfers.
221-Thank you for using the FTP service on ftp.cvshome.org.
221 Goodbye.
root@localhost$
#
```

Unpacking CVS

If you have GNU tar, use a single command to unpack CVS:

```
# cd /usr/local/src
# tar xvzf cvs-1.10.8.tar.gz
```

Otherwise, you need to use more commands:

```
# gunzip -c cvs-1.10.8.tar.gz | tar xvf -
```

In either case, you are left with the directory */usr/local/src/
cvs-1.10.8*, which contains the entire source distribution of
CVS.

Compiling CVS

The following example assumes you want to install CVS in
/usr/local:

```
# cd cvs-1.10.8
# ./configure --prefix /usr/local
# make
```

Installing CVS

The make install command installs the CVS programs and
documentation:

```
# make install
```

Once this is complete, other configuration steps may be necessary, such as downloading and installing the Secure Shell
(ssh) or setting up the *inetd.conf* so CVS can run in server
mode. See the following section for more information.

Administrator Reference

This section provides details on creating and configuring repositories and performing other CVS administrative tasks. A single computer can run multiple copies of the CVS server, and each server can serve multiple repositories.

Creating a Repository

Select a directory to contain the repository files (*/usr/local/cvs-rep* is used in the following examples). Use the init command to initialize the repository. Set the $CVSROOT environment variable first:

```
$ export CVSROOT=/usr/local/cvsrep
$ cvs init
```

Or use the -d option to specify the repository location:

```
$ cvs -d /usr/local/cvsrep init
```

For information on importing code, see the "User Reference" section, especially the "import" section and the "add" section.

Setting up the password server

If you want users to access the repository from other computers, configure the pserver by doing the following as root:

- Make sure there is an entry in */etc/services* similar to the following:

  ```
  cvspserver 2401/tcp
  ```

- If you don't use tcpwrappers, place a line like this in */etc/inetd.conf*:

  ```
  cvspserver stream tcp nowait root /usr/bin/cvs cvs↵
    --allow-root=/usr/local/cvsroot pserver
  ```

- If you use tcpwrappers, place a line like this:

  ```
  cvspserver stream tcp nowait root /usr/sbin/tcpd↵
    /usr/bin/cvs --allow-root=/usr/local/cvsroot pserver
  ```

- Once these changes are in place, restart `inetd` (or send it the appropriate signal to reread *inetd.conf*).

Security Issues

The following are security issues that need to be considered when working with CVS:

- The contents of files are transmitted in the open over the network with `pserver` and `rsh`. With `pserver`, passwords are transmitted in the open as well.

- When using a local repository (i.e., when CVS is not being used in client-server mode), developers need write-access to the repository, which means they can hack it.

- The CVS server runs as root briefly before changing its user ID.

- The `~/.cvspass` file must be kept unreadable by all users except the owner to prevent passwords from being accessible.

- A user who has authority to make changes to the files in the *CVSROOT* module can run arbitrary programs.

- Some options to the `admin` command are dangerous, so it is advisable to restrict its use. This can be accomplished by creating a user group named `cvsadmin`. If this user group exists, only users in that group can run the `admin` command (except `admin -kkflag`, which is available to everyone).

Repository Structure

The CVS repository is implemented as a normal directory with special contents. This section describes the contents of the repository directory. The repository format is compatible since CVS Version 1.6; see Cederqvist, et al. for information on older versions of CVS.

The CVSROOT Directory

The *CVSROOT* directory contains the administrative files for the repository; other directories in the repository contain the modules. The administrative files permit (and ignore) blank lines and comment lines in addition to the lines with real configuration information on them. Comment lines start with a hash mark (#).

Some of the administrative files contain filename patterns to match file and directory names. These patterns are regular expressions such as those used in GNU Emacs. Table 2 contains the special constructions used most often.

Table 2: Filename-Pattern Special Constructions

Construction	Description
^	Match the beginning of the string
$	Match the end of the string
.	Match any single character
*	Modify the preceding construct to match zero or more repetitions

CVS performs a few important expansions in the contents of the administrative files before interpreting the results. First, the typical shell syntax for referring to a home directory is ~/, which expands to the home directory of the user running CVS, and ~*user* expands to the home directory of the specified user.

In addition, CVS provides a mechanism similar to the shell's environment variable-expansion capability. Constructs such as ${*variable*} are replaced by the values of the named variables. Variable names start with letters and consist entirely of letters, numbers, and underscores. Curly brackets may be omitted if the character immediately following the variable reference is not a valid variable name character. While this construct looks like a shell environment variable reference, the full environment is not available. Table 3 contains the built-in variables.

Table 3: Administrative File Variables

Variable	Description
CVSEDITOR EDITOR VISUAL	The editor CVS uses for log file editing
CVSROOT	The repository locator in use
USER	The name of the user running CVS; if using a remote repository, the username must be known to the server
=var	The value of a user-defined variable named *var*; values for these variables are provided by the global -s option

To edit these files, check out the *CVSROOT* module from the repository, perform the edits, and commit them back to the repository. The changes must be committed for them to affect CVS's behavior.

Table 4 describes the administrative files and their functions.

Table 4: CVSROOT Files

File	Description
checkoutlist	Extra files to be maintained in *CVSROOT*
commitinfo	Specifications for commit governors
config	Settings to affect the behavior of CVS
cvsignore	Filename patterns of files to ignore
cvswrappers	Specifications for checkout and commit filters
editinfo	Specifications for log editors (obsolete)
history	Log information for the history command
loginfo	Specifies commit notifier program(s)
modules	Module definitions
notify	Notification processing specifications
passwd	A list of users and their CVS-specific passwords
rcsinfo	Template form for log messages
readers	A list of users having read-only access
taginfo	Tag processing specifications

File	Description
users	Alternate user email addresses for use with *notify*
verifymsg	Specifies log message evaluator program
writers	A list of users having read/write access

Since the *editinfo* file is obsolete, use the $EDITOR environment variable (or the -e option) to specify the editor and the *verifymsg* file to specify an evaluator.

Each line of the *taginfo* file contains a filename pattern and a command line to execute when files with matching names are tagged.

The checkoutlist file

Whenever changes to files in the *CVSROOT* module are committed, CVS prints the message:

```
cvs commit: Rebuilding administrative file database
```

to inform you that the checked-out copy in the repository has been updated to reflect any changes just committed. As with any other module directory in the repository, the *CVSROOT* directory contains RCS (*,v*) files that retain the history of the files. But to use the files, CVS needs a copy of the latest revision. So, when CVS prints this message, it is checking out the latest revisions of the administrative files.

If you have added files to the *CVSROOT* module (such as scripts to be called via entries in the *loginfo* file), you need to list them in the *checkoutlist* file. This makes CVS treat them the same way as it treats the standard set of *CVSROOT* files.

Each line in this file consists of a filename and an optional error message that displays in case there is trouble checking out the file.

The commitinfo file

Whenever a commit is being processed, CVS consults this file to determine whether or not any precommit checking of the file is required. Each line of the file contains a directory name pattern, followed by the path of a program to invoke when files are commited in directories with matching names.

Aside from the usual filename-pattern syntax, there are two special patterns:

ALL If this pattern is present in the file, then all files are passed to the specified checking program. CVS then looks for a pattern that matches the name of each particular file, and runs the additional checks found, if any.

DEFAULT

If this pattern is present in the file, all files for which there was no pattern match are sent to the specified checking program. The automatic match of every file to the ALL entry, if any, does not count as a match when determining whether or not to send the file to the DEFAULT checking program.

CVS constructs the command line for the checking program by appending the full path to the directory within the repository and the list of files being committed (this means you can specify the first few command-line arguments to the program, if necessary). If the checking program exits with a non-zero status, the commit is aborted.

The programs that run via this mechanism are run on the server computer when a remote repository is used. Here is an example of a *commitinfo* file:

```
ALL $CVSROOT/CVSROOT/commit-ALL.pl
DEFAULT $CVSROOT/CVSROOT/commit-DEFAULT.pl
CVSROOT$ $CVSROOT/CVSROOT/commit-CVSROOT.pl
```

This example assumes you will create the script files in the *CVSROOT* module and add them to the *checkoutlist* file.

The config file

Repository configuration is specified in the *config* administrative file.

LockDir=*dir*

> This directs CVS to put its lock files in the alternate directory given instead of in the repository itself, allowing users without write access to the repository (but with write access to *dir*) to read from the repository.

> Version 1.10 doesn't support alternate directories for lock files and reports an error if this option is set. Older versions of CVS (1.9 and older) don't support this option either and don't report an error. Do not mix versions that support alternate directories for lock files with versions that don't, since lock files in both places defeat the purpose of having them.

RCSBIN=*dir*

> Obsolete (used in Versions 1.9.12 to 1.9.18). This option used to tell CVS where to find RCS programs. Since all RCS-related functions are now handled internally, this option does nothing.

SystemAuth=*value*

> CVS tries to authenticate users via the *CVSROOT/passwd* file first, and if that fails and this option is set to yes, CVS tries to authenticate via the system's user database. This option is used with the password server. The default is yes.

TopLevelAdmin=*value*

> If this option is set to yes, an additional *CVS* directory is created at the top-level directory when checkout is run. This allows the client software to detect the repository locator in that directory (see the "Repository Locators" section). The default is no.

> This option is useful if you check out multiple modules to the same sandbox directory. If it is enabled, you won't have to provide a repository locator after the first

checkout; CVS infers it from the information in the top-level *CVS* directory created during the first checkout.

The cvsignore file

The *cvsignore* administrative file contains a list of filename patterns to ignore, just like the *.cvsignore* files that can appear in sandboxes and user home directories. Unlike the filename patterns in other administrative files, these patterns are in sh syntax; they are not GNU Emacs–style regular expressions. There can be multiple patterns on a line, separated by whitespace (consequently, the patterns themselves cannot contain whitespace).

Table 5 shows the most commonly used sh-style pattern constructs.

Table 5: Filename Patterns for cvsignore

Construct	Description
?	Any one character
*	Any sequence of zero or more characters

Again diverging from the standards used by the rest of the administrative files, the *cvsignore* file does not support comments.

The cvswrappers file

While the *cvsignore* file directs CVS to ignore certain files, the *cvswrappers* file allows you to give CVS default options for commands that work with files. Lines in this file consist of a sh-style filename pattern followed by a -k (keyword substitution mode) option and/or an -m (update method) option. The legal values for -k are described in Table 19. The legal values for -m are COPY and MERGE.

If -m COPY is specified, CVS doesn't attempt to merge the files. Instead, it presents the user with conflicting versions of the file, and he can choose one or the other, or resolve the conflict manually.

For example, to treat all files ending in *.exe* as binary, add this line to the file:

```
*.exe -k b
```

The history file

If this file exists, CVS inserts records of activity occurring in the repository. This information produces displays of the `cvs history` command. The *history* file is not intended for direct reading or writing by programs other than CVS.

A repository set up with `cvs init` automatically has a *history* file.

The loginfo file

The *loginfo* administrative file works much like the *commitinfo* file and can use the special patterns `ALL` and `DEFAULT`. This file allows you to do something with `commit` log messages and related information.

The programs called during *loginfo* processing receive the log message on standard input. Table 6 shows the three codes that can pass additional information to the called programs via command-line arguments.

Table 6: Special loginfo Variables

Variable	Description
s	Filename
V	Precommit revision number
v	Post-commit revision number

If a percent sign (%) followed by the desired variable is placed after the command path, CVS inserts the corresponding information as a whitespace-separated list with one entry for each file, preceded by the repository path (as with *commitinfo*). There can be only one percent sign on the command line, so if you want information from more than one variable, place the variable names inside curly brackets: %{...}. In this case, each file-specific entry has one field for each variable, separated by commas. For example, the code %{sVv} expands to a list like this:

```
/usr/local/cvsrep/hello Makefile,1.1,1.2 hello.c,1.8,1.9
```

It can be helpful to send email notifications each time someone commits a file to the repository. Developers can monitor this stream of notices to determine when they should pull the latest development code into their private sandboxes. For example, consider a developer doing some preparatory work in his sandbox while he awaits stabilization and addition of another developer's new library. As soon as the new library is added and committed, email notification goes out, and the waiting developer sees the code is ready to use. So he runs cvs upd -d in the appropriate directory to pull in the new library code and then sets about integrating it with his work.

It is simple to set up this kind of notification. Just add a line like this to the *CVSROOT/loginfo* file:

```
DEFAULT mail -s %s developers@company.com
```

Often, the email address is a mailing list, which has all the interested parties (developers or otherwise) on the distribution list. If you want to send messages to multiple email addresses, you can write a script to do that and have that script called via this file. Alternatively, you can use the log.pl program that comes as part of the CVS source distribution (located at */usr/local/src/cvs-1.10.8/contrib/log.pl*, assuming CVS was unpacked into */usr/local/src*). Instructions for its use are provided as comments in the file.

The modules file

The top-level directories in a repository are called *modules*. In addition to these physical modules, CVS provides a mechanism to create logical modules through the *modules* administrative file. Here are the three kinds of logical modules:

Alias

Alias modules are defined by lines of the form:

```
module_name -a alias_module ...
```

The effect of using an alias module name in a CVS command is exactly the same as specifying the modules listed after the -a option on the command line.

Regular

Regular modules are defined by lines of the form:

```
module_name [options] directory file ...
```

Checking out *module_name* results in the specified files from *directory* being checked out into a directory named *module_name*. The intervening directories (if any) are not reflected in the sandbox.

Ampersand

Ampersand modules are defined by lines of the form:

```
module_name [options] &other_module ...
```

Checking out such a module results in a directory named *module_name*, which in turn contains copies of the *other_module* modules.

Table 7 shows the options that can define modules.

Table 7: Module Options

Option	Description
-d *name*	Overrides the default working directory name for the module
-e *prog*	Runs the program *prog* when files are exported from the module; the module name is passed to *prog* as the sole argument
-i *prog*	Run the program *prog* when files are committed to the module; the repository directory of the committed files is passed to *prog* as the sole argument

Table 7: Module Options (continued)

Option	Description
-i *prog*	Run the program *prog* when files are checked out from the module; the module name is passed to *prog* as the sole argument
-s *status*	Assign a status descriptor to the module
-t *prog*	Run the program *prog* when files are tagged in the module using rtag; the module name and the symbolic tag are passed to *prog*
-u *prog*	Run the program *prog* when files are updated in the module's top-level directory; the absolute path to the module within the repository is passed to *prog* as the sole argument

Alias modules provide alternative names for other modules or shortcuts for referring to collections or subdirectories of other modules. Alias-module definitions function like macro definitions in that they cause commands to run as if the expanded list of modules and directories was on the command line. Alias modules do not cause the modules of their definition to be grouped together under the alias name (use ampersand modules for that). For example, the definition:

```
h -a hello
```

makes the name *h* a synonym for the *hello* module. This definition:

```
project -a library client server
```

allows you to check out all three modules of the project as a unit. If an entry in the definition of an alias module is preceded by an exclamation point (!), the named directory is excluded from the module.

Regular modules allow you to create modules that are subsets of other modules. For example, the definition:

```
header library library.h
```

creates a module that contains just the header file from the *library* module.

Ampersand modules are true logical modules. There are no top-level directories for them in the repository, but you can check them out to sandboxes, and directories with their names will then appear. The modules listed in the definition are below the directory. For example:

```
project &library &client &server
```

is almost the same as the alias module example given earlier, except that the submodules are checked out inside a subdirectory named *project*.

In this file, long definitions may be split across multiple lines by terminating all but the last line with backslashes (\).

The notify file

This file is used in conjunction with the `watch` command. When notifications are appropriate, this file is consulted to determine how to do the notification.

Each line of the *notify* file contains a filename pattern and a command line. CVS's notification mechanism uses the command line specified to perform notifications for files having names that match the corresponding pattern.

There is a single special-purpose variable, `%s`, that can appear in the command specification. When the command is executed, the name of the user to notify replaces the variable name. If the *users* administrative file exists, the usernames are looked up there, and the resulting values are used for `%s` instead. This allows emails to be sent to accounts other than those on the local machine. Details are sent to the notification program via standard input.

Typical usage of this feature is the single entry:

```
ALL mail %s -s "CVS notification"
```

In fact, this entry is present in the default *notify* file created when you run `cvs init` to create a repository (although it is initially commented out).

The passwd file

If you access the repository via a `pserver` repository locator (see the "Repository Locators" section), CVS can have its own private authentication information, separate from the system's user database. This information is stored in the *CVSROOT/passwd* administrative file.

This feature provides anonymous CVS access over the Internet. By creating an entry for a public user (usually `anoncvs` or `anonymous`), the `pserver` can be used by many people sharing the public account. If you don't want to create a system user with the same name as the public user, or if you have such a user but it has a different purpose, you can employ a user alias to map it to something else:

```
anonymous:TY7QWpLw8bvus:cvsnoname
```

Then, make sure you create the `cvsnoname` user on the system. You can use */bin/false* as the login shell and the repository's root directory as the home directory for the user.

To restrict the public user to read-only access, list it in the *CVSROOT/readers* administrative file.

Additionally, CVS's private user database is useful even if you don't want to set up anonymous CVS access. You can restrict access to a subset of the system's users, provide remote access to users who don't have general system access, or prevent a user's normal system password from being transmitted in the clear over the network (see the "Security Issues" section).

There is no `cvs passwd` command for setting CVS-specific passwords (located in repository file *CVSROOT/passwd*). CVS-specific user and password management are manual tasks.

The rcsinfo file

CVS consults this file when doing a commit or import to determine the log message editor template. Each entry in the file consists of a filename pattern and the name of the file to use as the template for module directories with matching names.

The ALL and DEFAULT special patterns apply to this file.

The readers file

Users listed in this file (if it exists) will have read-only access.

The taginfo file

CVS consults this administrative file whenever the tag or rtag commands are used. Entries in this file are filename patterns and program specifications. The ALL special pattern applies to this file.

The *taginfo* file is called with the tag, the operation being performed, the module directory name (relative to the repository root), and the filename and revision number for each affected file. The valid operations are: add (for tag), del (for tag -d), and mov (for tag -F).

If the *taginfo* program returns a non-zero status, the tag or rtag command that caused its execution is aborted.

The users file

If this file exists, it is consulted during processing of the *notify* administrative file's contents. Entries in this file consist of two colon-separated fields on a single line. The first field is the name of a user, and the second field is a value (normally the user's email address on another machine). For example:

```
john:john@somecompany.com
jane:jane@anothercompany.com
```

The verifymsg file

CVS consults this file to determine if log messages should be validated. If the program returns a non-zero status, the commit is aborted. The *verifymsg* file is called with the absolute path to a file containing the log message to be verified.

The ALL special pattern is not supported for this file, although DEFAULT is. If more than one pattern matches, the first match is used.

The writers file

If this file exists, users listed in it have read/write access (unless they are also listed in the *readers* file, in which case they have read-only access).

Hacking the Repository

Since the repository is a normal directory—albeit one with special contents—it is possible to cd to the directory to examine its contents or make changes to its files and directories. For each file that has been added, there is a file with the same name followed by ",v" in a corresponding directory in the repository. These are RCS (the format, not the program) files that contain multiple versions of the file.

Since the activities discussed in this section involve making changes directly to the repository instead of working through CVS commands, you should exercise extreme caution and have current backups.

Restructuring a project

Restructuring the project by moving files and directories around (and possibly renaming them) in the repository allows the files to retain their history. The standard way to rename a file using CVS is to rename the file in the sandbox, and do a cvs remove on the old name and a cvs add on the new name. However, this results in the file being disconnected from its history under the new name, so sometimes it is better

---

to do the renaming directly in the repository. Note that doing this while people have active sandboxes is dangerous, since the sandboxes will contain information about a file that is no longer in the repository.

Bulk importing

When importing an entire project, all the project's files are added to the repository. But if some of these files shouldn't have been added, you'll want to remove them. Doing a `cvs remove` accomplishes this, but copies of those files remain in the repository's *.Attic* directory forever. To avoid this, delete the files from the repository directly before checking out sandboxes from it.

Importing

If you have an existing code base, you'll want to import it into CVS in a way that preserves the most historical information. This section provides instructions for importing projects into CVS from code snapshots or other version-control systems. All of these (except the code snaphot import procedure) are based on conversion to RCS files, followed by placing the RCS files in the proper location in the CVS repository.

Importing code snapshots

If you maintain project history archives manually by taking periodic snapshots of the code, you can import the first snapshot, tag it with the date or version number, and then successively overlay the updated files from later archives. Each set can then be committed and tagged in order to bootstrap a repository that maintains the prior history.

For example, first unpack the distributions (this assumes they unpack to directories containing the version numbers):

```
$ tar xvzf foo-1.0.tar.gz
$ tar xvzf foo-1.1.tar.gz
$ tar xvzf foo-2.0.tar.gz
```

Next, make a copy of the first version, import it into the CVS repository, check it out to make a sandbox (since importing doesn't convert the source directory into a sandbox), and use cvs tag to give it a symbolic name reflecting the project version:

```
$ mkdir foo
$ cp -R -p foo-1.0/* foo
$ cd foo
$ cvs import -m 'Imported version 1.0' foo↵
  vendor start
$ cd ..
$ mv foo foo.bak
$ cvs checkout foo
$ cd foo
$ cvs tag foo-1_0
$ cd ..
```

Next, apply the differences between Version 1.0 and 1.1 to the sandbox, commit the changes, and create a tag:

```
$ diff -Naur foo-1.0 foo-1.1 | (cd foo; patch↵
  -Np1)
$ cd foo
$ cvs commit -m 'Imported version 1.1'
$ cvs tag foo-1_1
$ cd ..
```

In the same way, apply the differences between Version 1.1 and 2.0 to the sandbox, commit the changes, and create a tag:

```
$ diff -Naur foo-1.1 foo-2.0 | (cd foo; patch↵
  -Np1)
$ cd foo
$ cvs commit -m 'Imported version 2.0'
$ cvs tag foo-2_0
```

Now you can use the log to view the history of the files, browse past versions of the files, and continue development under version control.

Importing from RCS

If you migrate from RCS to CVS, following these next instructions results in a usable CVS repository. This procedure involves direct modification of the CVS repository, so it should be undertaken with caution.

Before beginning, make sure none of the files to be imported into CVS are locked by RCS. Then, create a new CVS repository and module (or a new module within an existing repository). Next, create directories in the CVS repository to mirror the project's directory structure. Finally, copy all the version files (,v) from the project (which may be in *RCS* subdirectories) into the appropriate directories in the repository (without *RCS* subdirectories).

For example, first move aside the directory under RCS control, create an empty directory to build the new CVS structure, import the directory, then check it out to make a sandbox:

```
$ mv foo foo-rcs
$ mkdir foo
$ cd foo
$ cvs import -m 'New empty project' foo vendor↵
  start
$ cd ..
$ mv foo foo.bak
$ cvs checkout foo
```

Next, make directories and add them to the repository to match the structure in the RCS project:

```
$ cd foo
$ mkdir dir
$ cvs add dir
$ cd ..
```

Now, copy the *,v* files from the RCS project into the repository for the CVS project:

```
$ cp -p foo-rcs/*,v $CVSROOT/foo
$ cp -p foo-rcs/dir/*,v $CVSROOT/foo/dir
```

Finally, issue the `cvs update` command in the sandbox directory to bring in the latest versions of all the files:

```
$ cd foo
$ cvs upd
```

Importing from SCCS

To import from SCCS, use the `sccs2rcs` script (located in the
contrib directory of the CVS distribution) to convert the files
to RCS format, and then follow the RCS procedure described
in the previous section. Both CVS and SCCS must be installed
for this to work. The script's comments contain additional
instructions.

Importing from PVCS

To import from PVCS, use the `pvcs_to_rcs` script (located in
the *contrib* directory of the CVS distribution) to convert the
files to RCS format, and then follow the RCS procedure
described in the "Importing from RCS" section. Both CVS and
PVCS must be installed for this to work. The script's comments contain additional instructions.

Using an Interim Shared Sandbox

Over time, projects may develop unintended environmental
dependencies, especially when there is no pressure for the
code to be relocatable. A project developed outside version
control may even be initially developed in-place (at its
intended installation location). While these practices are not
recommended, they do occur in the real world; CVS can help
to improve the situation by encouraging relocatability from
the beginning of a project.

The default mode of operation for CVS is multiple independent sandboxes, all coordinated with a central shared repository. Code that runs in this environment is necessarily (at least
partially) relocatable. So, using CVS from the beginning of a
project helps ensure flexibility.

However, if a project is already well underway, an interim approach can be used. For example, you can convert the development area to a single shared sandbox by importing the code into CVS and checking it back out again:

```
$ cd /usr/local/bar
$ cvs import bar vendor start
$ cd ..
$ mv bar bar.bak
$ cvs checkout bar
```

Chances are good that this approach is too aggressive and will check in more files than absolutely necessary. You can either go back and hack the repository to remove the files that shouldn't be there or just issue the cvs remove command to delete them as you discover them.

In addition, there will probably be some binary files in the sandbox that were imported as text files. Wherever you see a binary file that needs to remain in the repository, you should issue the command cvs admin -kb file, then make a fresh copy from the project backup. Finally, issue the command cvs commit file to commit the fixed file back to the repository.

Having version control in place before making flexibility enhancements is a good idea, since it makes it easier to find (and possibly reverse) changes that cause trouble.

The repository locator (see the "Repository Locators" section) is specified via the -d option or the $CVSROOT environment variable. It is stored in the various sandbox *CVS/root* files. If you use the Password Server (pserver), the user ID of the person checking out the sandbox is retained. If more than one person is working with a particular sandbox, they have to share an account for CVS access.

One way to do this is to have a neutral user account with a password known by everyone with CVS access. Anyone can then issue the cvs login command with the same user ID and password, and access the repository. Once you stop using a shared sandbox, you won't need this workaround. However, while you're using a shared sandbox, it's important that

---

developers type their real user IDs into their log messages, since all the changes will appear to be made by the common user.

Global Server Option

The server has one global option, `--allow-root=rootdir`. This option tells the CVS server to accept and process requests for the specified repository.

Administrator Commands

Table 8 lists the commands that CVS administrators can use to manage their repositories.

Table 8: Administrator Commands

Command	Description
admin adm rcs	Perform administrative functions
init	Create a new repository
server	Run in server mode

admin

```
admin
  [ -b[rev] ]
  [ -cstring ]
  [ -kkflag ]
  [ -l[rev] ]
  [ -L ]
  [ -mrev:msg ]
  [ -nname[:[rev]] ]
  [ -Nname[:[rev]] ]
  [ -orange ]
  [ -q ]
  [ -sstate[:rev] ]
  [ -t[file] ]
  [ -t-string ]
```

```
[ -u[rev] ]
[ -U ]
[ files ... ]
```

The admin performs administrative functions. If a cvsadmin
user group exists, only those users in that group can run
admin with options other than -k. Additional options that may
be used with the admin command are listed in Table 9.

Table 9: admin Options

Option	Description
-b[rev]	Set the default branch
-cstring	Obsolete; set the comment leader
-kkflag	Set the default keyword substitution mode
-l[rev]	Lock the specified revision
-L	Enable strict locking
-mrev:msg	Change the revision's log message
-nname[:[rev]]	Associate the symbolic *name* with the branch or revision specified
-Nname[:[rev]]	The same as -n, except that if *name* is already in use, the new one is moved
-orange	Delete revisions permanently
-q	Don't print diagnostics
-sstate[:rev]	Change the state of a revision
-t[file]`	Set the descriptive text in the RCS file(s)
-t-string	Set the descriptive text in the RCS file(s) to *string*
-u[rev]	Unlock the specified revision
-U	Disable strict locking

If the revision specified for -l is a branch, the latest revision
on that branch is used. If no revision is given, the latest revision on the default branch is used.

If the name given for -n is already in use, an error is generated. You can use -N to move a tag (change the revision asso-
ciated with the tag); however, you should use cvs tag or cvs
rtag instead.

The -o option is dangerous and results in a permanent loss of information from the repository. Use it with extreme caution and only after careful consideration. See Table 10 for the various ways to specify ranges. There must not be any branches or locks on the revisions to be removed. Beware of interactions between this command and symbolic names.

If no *file* is specified to the -t option, CVS reads from standard input until it reaches the end of the file or a period on a line by itself.

The determination of the target revision for the -u option is the same as for -l.

Table 10: Range Formats

Format	Description
rev1::*rev2*	Eliminate versions between *rev1* and *rev2*, retaining only enough information to go directly from *rev1* to *rev2*; the two specified versions are retained
::*rev*	The same as *rev1*::*rev2*, except the first revision is the branchpoint revision
rev::	The same as *rev1*::*rev2*, except the second revision is the end of the branch, and it is deleted instead of retained
rev	Delete the specified revision
rev1:*rev2*	The same as *rev1*::*rev2*, except the two named revisions are deleted as well
:*rev*	The same as ::*rev*, except the named revision is deleted as well
rev:	The same as *rev*::, except the named revision is deleted as well

The options in Table 11 are present in CVS for historical reasons and should not be used. Using these options may corrupt the repository.

Table 11: Obsolete admin Options

Option	Description
-a*logins*	Appended the logins to the access list of the RCS file
-A*oldfile*	Appended the access list of *oldfile* to the access list of the RCS file
-e[*logins*]	Erased logins from the RCS file's access list, or erased all if a list is not provided
-i	Created and initialized a new RCS file; instead of using this option, use add to add files to a CVS repository
-I	Ran interactively; this option doesn't work with client-server CVS, and is likely to be removed in a future version
-V*n*	Specified that the RCS files used by CVS should be compatible with a specific version of RCS
-x*suffixes*	Used to determine the filename suffix for RCS files, but CVS uses only ,v as the RCS file suffix

init

init

The init command initializes the repository. Use the global -d option to specify the repository's directory if $CVSROOT isn't set appropriately.

The newly initialized repository contains a CVSROOT module, but nothing else. Once the repository is initialized, you can add files to it or check out the CVSROOT module to make changes to the administrative files by using other CVS commands.

pserver

pserver

This command tells CVS to operate as a server, providing access to the repositories specified before the command with the --allow-root option. This command is used in the *inetd.conf* file, not on the command line. Another global option frequently used with this command is -T (see Table 1).

User Reference

This section provides details on connecting to a repository, the structure of sandboxes, and using CVS commands.

Repository Locators

CVS currently supports five methods for the client to access the repository: Local connection, External connection, Password Server, GSS-API (Generic Security Services API) Server, and Kerberos 4 Server (most Kerberos users will want to use GSS-API). Table 12 describes the various repository locator types and their respective access methods.

Table 12: Repository Access Types and Methods

Method	Locator Format	Description
Local	*path* :local:*path*	If the repository directory is local to the computer from which you will access it (or appears local, as with an NFS or Samba mounted filesystem), the repository string is just the path name of the repository directory, such as */usr/local/cvsrep* or it can use the :local: prefix.
External	:ext:*user@host:path*	External repositories are accessed via a remote shell utility, usually rsh (the default) or ssh. The environment variable $CVS_RSH specifies the remote shell program.

Method	Locator Format	Description
Password Server	`:pserver:`*`user@host:path`*	Password Server repositories require authentication to a user account before you can use the repository. Public CVS servers are commonly configured this way so they can provide anonymous CVS access. See the "The passwd file" section for more information on anonymous CVS.
GSS-API Server	`:gserver:`	This locator type is used for servers accessible via Kerberos 5 or other authentication mechanisms supported by GSS-API.
Kerberos Server	`:kserver:`	This locator type is used for servers accessible via Kerberos 4.

Configuring CVS

CVS's behavior can be influenced by two classes of settings other than the command-line arguments: *environment variables* (see Table 13) and *special files* (see Table 14).

Table 13: Environment Variables

Variable	Description
$COMSPEC	Command interpreter on OS/2, if not cmd.exe.
$CVS_CLIENT_LOG	Client-side debugging file specification for client-server connections. $CVS_CLIENT_LOG is the basename for the *$CVS_CLIENT_LOG.in* and *$CVS_CLIENT_LOG.out* files, which will be written in the current working directory at the time a command is executed.
$CVS_CLIENT_PORT	The port number for :kserver: locators. $CVS_CLIENT_PORT doesn't need to be set if the kserver is listening on port 1999 (the default).
$CVS_IGNORE_REMOTE_ROOT	According to the *ChangeLog*, this variable was removed from CVS with version 1.10.3.
$CVS_PASSFILE	Password file for :pserver: locators. This variable must be set before issuing the cvs login to have the desired effect. Defaults to *$HOME/.cvspass*.
$CVS_RCMD_PORT	For non-Unix clients, the port for connecting to the server's rcmd daemon.
$CVS_RSH	Remote shell for :ext: locators, if not rsh.
$CVS_SERVER	Remote server program for :ext: locators, if not cvs.

Table 13: Environment Variables (continued)

Variable	Description
$CVS_SERVER_SLEEP	Server-side execution delay (in seconds) to allow time to attach a debugger.
$CVSEDITOR	Editor used for log messages; overrides $EDITOR.
$CVSIGNORE	A list of filename patterns to ignore, separated by whitespace. (See also *cvsignore* in Table 4 and *.cvsignore* in Table 14.)
$CVSREAD	Determines read-only (if the variable is set) or read/write (if the variable is not set) for checkout and update.
$CVSROOT	Default repository locator.
$CVSUMASK	Determines permissions for (local) repository files.
$CVSWRAPPERS	A list of filename patterns for the *cvswrappers* function. See also the "Repository Structure" section.
$EDITOR	Specifies the editor to use for log messages; see notes for $CVSEDITOR.
$HOME	On Unix, used to find the *.cvsrc* file.
$HOMEDRIVE	On Windows NT, used to find the *.cvsrc* file.
$HOMEPATH	On Windows NT, used to find the *.cvsrc* file.
$PATH	Used to locate programs to run.
$RCSBIN	Obsolete. Used to locate RCS programs to run.

Variable	Description
$TEMP $TMP $TMPDIR	Location for temporary files. $TMPDIR is used by the server. On Unix, */tmp* (and TMP on Windows NT) may not be overridden for some functions of CVS due to reliance on the system's tmpnam( ) function.

Despite the similarity in names, the $CVSROOT environment variable and the *CVSROOT* directory in a repository are not related to each other.

The "RSH" in the name of the $CVS_RSH environment variable doesn't refer to the particular program (rsh), but rather to the program CVS is using to create remote shell connections (which could be some program other than rsh, such as ssh).

Since there is only one way to specify the remote shell program to use ($CVS_RSH) and this is a global setting, users that commonly access multiple repositories need to pay close attention to which repository they are using. If one repository requires one setting of this variable and another requires a different setting, this variable needs to be changed between accesses to these repositories. This aspect of the repository access method is not stored in the *CVS/Root* file in the sandbox (see the "CVS directories" section). For example, if you access some repositories via rsh and some via ssh, you can create the following two utility aliases (assuming CVS is installed in */usr/local/bin*):

```
user@localhost$ alias cvs="export CVS_RSH=ssh; cvs"
user@localhost$ alias cvr="export CVS_RSH=rsh; cvs"
```

Table 14 shows the files used by the CVS command-line client for server connection and client configuration information. These files reside in the user's home directory.

Table 14: Client Configuration Files

Option	Description
~/.cvsignore	Filename patterns of files to ignore
~/.cvspass	Passwords cached by cvs login
~/.cvsrc	Default command options
~/.cvswrappers	User-specific checkout and commit filters

The *~/.cvspass* file is really an operational file, not a configuration file. It is used by the cvs client program to store the repository user account password between cvs login and cvs logoff.

Some common *.cvsrc* settings are:

```
update -dP
```
Brings in new directories and prunes empty directories on cvs update

```
diff -c
```
Gives output in context diff format

Creating a Sandbox

In order to use CVS, you must create a sandbox or have one created for you. This section describes sandbox creation, assuming there is already a module in the repository you want to work with (see the "import" section for information on importing a new module into the repository):

- Determine the repository locator. Talk to the repository administrator if you need help finding the repository or getting the locator syntax right.

- If this will be the main repository you use, set $CVSROOT. Otherwise, use the -d option when running CVS commands that don't infer the repository from the sandbox files.

- Pick a module to check out.

- Pick a sandbox location and `cd` to the parent directory.

- If the repository requires login, do `cvs login`.

- Run `cvs checkout` *module*.

For example:

```
export CVSROOT=/usr/local/cvsroot
cd ~/work
cvs checkout hello
```

Sandbox Structure

This section describes the files and directories that may be encountered in sandboxes.

.cvsignore files

Sandboxes may contain *.cvsignore* files. These files specify filename patterns for files that may exist in the sandbox but normally aren't checked into CVS. This is commonly used to cause CVS to bypass derived files.

.cvswrappers files

Sandboxes may contain *.cvswrappers* files. These provide directory-specific file handling information like that in the repository configuration file *cvswrappers* (see the "The cvswrappers file" section).

CVS directories

Each directory in a sandbox contains a *CVS* directory. The files in this directory (see Table 15) contain metadata used by CVS to locate the repository and track which file versions have been copied to the sandbox.

Table 15: Files in the CVS Directories

File	Description
Base *Baserev* *Baserev.tmp*	The *Base* directory stores copies of files when the `edit` command is in use; the *Baserev* file contains the revision numbers of the files in *Base*; the *Baserev.tmp* file is used in updating the *Baserev* file.
Checkin.prog *Update.prog*	The programs specified in the *modules* file for options -i and -u, respectively.
Entries	Version numbers and timestamps for the files as they were copied from the repository when checked out or updated.
Entries.Backup *Entries.Log* *Entries.Static*	Temporary and intermediate files used by CVS.
Notify *Notify.tmp*	Temporary files used by CVS for dealing with notifications for commands such as `edit` and `unedit`.
Repository	The name by which the directory is known in the repository.
Root	The repository locator in effect when the sandbox was created (via `cvs checkout`).
Tag	Information about sticky tags and dates for files in the directory.
Template	Stores the contents of the *rcsinfo* administrative file from the repository for remote repositories.

Since each sandbox directory has one *CVS/Root* file, a sandbox directory corresponds to exactly one repository. You cannot check out some files from one repository and some from another into a single sandbox directory.

Client Global Options

Table 16 lists the global options that control the operation of the CVS client program.

Table 16: Client Global Options

Option	Description
-a	Authenticate (gserver only)
-d root	Locate the repository; overrides the setting of $CVSROOT
-e editor	Specify message editor; overrides the settings of $CVSEDITOR and $EDITOR
-f	Don't read `~/.cvsrc`; useful when you have *.cvsrc* settings you want to forego for a particular command
-H [command] --help [command]	Display help; if no command is specified, general CVS help (including a list of other help options) is displayed
-l	Don't log command in history
-n	Don't change any files; useful when you want to know ahead of time which files will be affected by a particular command
-q	Be quiet
-Q	Be very quiet; only prints messages for serious problems
-r	Make new working files read-only
-s variable=value	Set the value of a user variable to a given value; user variables can be used in the contents of administrative files
-t	Trace execution; helpful in debugging remote repository connection problems and, in conjunction with -n, in determining the effect of an unfamiliar command

Option	Description
-w	Make new working files read/write; overrides $CVSREAD; files are read/write unless $CVSREAD is set or if -r is specified
-x	Encrypt (Introduced in Version 1.10)
-z gzip_level	Set the compression level; useful when using CVS in client-server mode across slow connections

Common Client Options

Tables 17 and 18 describe the options common to many CVS commands. Table 17 lists the options and describes their function, while Table 18 lists which options can be used with the user commands. Details will be provided in the sections that follow only for options that require further explanation.

Table 17: Common Options

Option	Description
-D date	Use the most recent revision no later than *date*
-f	For commands that involve tags (via -r) or dates (via -D), include the most recent revisions of each file that is not tagged with the specified tag or was not present on the specified date
-k kflag	Determine how to perform keyword substitution; the space between -k and *kflag* is optional (see Table 19 for the list of keyword substitution modes)
-l	Do not recurse into subdirectories
-n	Don't run module programs
-R	Do recurse into subdirectories (the default)
-r rev	Use a particular revision number or symbolic tag

Table 18 shows which common options are applicable to each user command.

Table 18: Client Common Option Applicability

User Command	-D	-f	-k	-l	-n	-R	-r
add			•				
annotate	•	•		•		•	•
checkout	•	•	•	•	•	•	•
commit				•	•	•	•
diff	•		•	•		•	•
edit				•		•	
editors				•		•	
export	•	•	•	•	•	•	•
help							
history	•						•
import			•				
log				•		•	
login							
logout							
rdiff	•	•		•		•	•
release							
remove				•		•	
rtag	•	•		•		•	•
status				•		•	
tag				•		•	
unedit				•		•	

User Command	-D	-f	-k	-l	-n	-R	-r
update	•	•	•	•		•	•
watch				•		•	
watchers				•		•	

Date formats

CVS understands dates in a variety of formats, including:

ISO standard
YYYY-MM-DD HH:MM. This is the preferred format, which reads as 2000-05-17 or 2000-05-17 22:00. The technical details of the format are defined in the ISO-8601 standard.

Email standard
17 May 2000. The technical details of the format are defined in the RFC-822 and RFC-1123 standards.

Relative
10 days ago, 4 years ago.

Common
month/day/year. This form can cause confusion because not all cultures use the first two fields in this order (1/2/2000 is ambiguous).

Other
Other formats are accepted, including YYYY/MM/DD and those omitting the year (which is assumed to be the current year).

Keyword substitutions

Table 19 describes the keyword substitution modes that can be selected with the -k option. CVS uses keyword substitutions to insert revision information into files when they are checked out or updated.

Table 19: Keyword Substitution Modes

Mode	Description
b	Binary mode. Treat the file the same as with mode o, but also avoid newline conversion.
k	Keyword-only mode. Flatten all keywords to just the keyword name. Use this mode if you want to compare two revisions of a file without seeing the keyword substitution differences.
kv	Keyword-value mode. The keyword and the corresponding value are substituted. This is the default mode.
kvl	Keyword-value-locker mode. This mode is the same as kv mode, except it always adds the lock holder's user ID if the revision is locked. The lock is obtained via the cvs admin -l command.
o	Old-contents mode. Use the keyword values as they appear in the repository rather than generating new values.
v	Value-only mode. Substitute the value of each keyword for the entire keyword field, omitting even the $ delimiters. This mode destroys the field in the process, so use it cautiously.

Keyword substitution fields are strings of the form $*Keyword* ...$. The valid keywords are:

Author

> The user ID of the person who committed the revision.

Date

> The date and time (in standard UTC format) the revision was committed.

Header

> The absolute path of the repository RCS file, the revision number, the commit date, time, and user ID, the file's state, and the lock holder's user ID if the file is locked.

Id A shorter form of Header, omitting the leading directory name(s) from the RCS file's path, leaving only the filename.

Name

The tag name that was used to retrieve the file; empty if no explicit tag was given when the file was retrieved.

Locker

The user ID of the user holding a lock on the file; empty if the file is not locked.

Log The RCS filename. In addition to keyword expansion in the keyword field, each commit inserts additional lines in the file immediately following the line containing this keyword. The first such line contains the revision number, the commit date, time, and user ID. Subsequent lines are the contents of the commit log message. The result over time is a reverse-chronological list of log entries for the file. Each additional line is preceded by the same characters that precede the keyword field on its line. This allows the log information to be formatted in a comment for most languages. For example:

```
#
# foo.pl
#
# $Log: foo.pl,v $
# Revision 1.2  2000/06/09 22:10:23  me
# Fixed the new bug introduced when the last one was fixed.
#
# Revision 1.1  2000/06/09 18:07:51  me
# Fixed the last remaining bug in the system.
#
```

Be sure not to place any keyword fields in your log messages if you use this keyword, since CVS will expand them if you do.

RCSfile

The name of the RCS file (without any leading directories).

Revision
  The revision number of the file.

Source
  The absolute path of the RCS file.

State
  The file's state, as assigned by `cvs admin -s` (if you don't
  set the state explicitly, it is Exp by default).

User Commands

The CVS client program provides the user commands defined
in Table 20.

Table 20: User Commands

Command	Description
ad add new	Indicate that files/directories should be added to the repository
ann annotate	Display contents of the head revision of a file, annotated with the revision number, user, and date of the last change for each line
checkout co get	Create a sandbox for a module
ci com commit	Commit changes from the sandbox back to the repository
di dif diff	View differences between file versions
edit	Prepare to edit files; used for enhanced developer coordination

Command	Description
editors	Display a list of users working on the files; used for enhanced developer coordination
ex exp export	Retrieve a module, but don't make the result a sandbox
help	Get help
hi his history	Display the log information for files
im imp import	Import new modules into the repository
lgn login logon	Log in to (cache the password for) a remote CVS server
lo log rlog	Show the activity log for the file(s)
logout	Log off from (flush the password for) a remote CVS server
pa patch rdiff	Release diff; the output is the format of input to Larry Wall's patch command; does not have to be run from within a sandbox
re rel release	Perform a logged delete on a sandbox

Table 20: User Commands (continued)

Command	Description
remove rm delete	Remove a file or directory from the repository
rt rtag rfreeze	Tag a particular revision
st stat status	Show detailed status for files
ta tag freeze	Attach a tag to files in the repository
unedit	Abandon file modifications and make read-only again
up upd update	Synchronize sandbox to repository
watch	Manage the watch settings; used for enhanced developer coordination
watchers	Display the list of users watching for changes to the files; used for enhanced developer coordination

add

```
add
  [ -k kflag ]
  [ -m message ]
  file ...
```

This command indicates that files/directories should be added to the repository. They are not actually added until they are committed via cvs commit. This command can also resurrect files deleted with cvs remove.

The standard meaning of the common client option -k applies. There is only one additional option that can be used with the add command: -m *message*. This option provides a description of the file (which appears in the output of the log command).

annotate

```
annotate
  [ [ -D date | -r rev ] -f ]
  [ -l | -R ]
  file ...
```

CVS prints a report showing each line of the specified file. Each line is prefixed by information about the most recent change to the line, including the revision number, the user, and the date. If no revision is specified, the head of the trunk revision of the trunk branch is used.

The standard meanings of the common client options -D, -f, -l, -r, and -R apply.

checkout

```
checkout
  [ -A ]
  [ -c | -s ]
  [ -d dir [ -N ] ]
  [ [ -D date | -r rev ] -f ]
  [ -j rev1 [ -j rev2 ] ]
  [ -k kflag ]
  [ -l | -R ]
  [ -n ]
  [ -p ]
  [ -P ]
  [ module ... ]
```

This command copies files from the repository to the sandbox.

The standard meanings of the common client options -D, -f, -k, -l, -r, and -R apply. Additional options are listed in Table 21.

Table 21: checkout Options

Option	Description
-A	Reset any sticky tags or dates
-c	Copy the *module* file to standard output
-d *dir*	Override the default directory name
-j *rev*	Join branches together
-N	Don't shorten module paths
-p	Pipe the files to standard output, with header lines between them showing the filename, RCS filename, and version
-P	Prune empty directories
-s	Show status for each module from the *modules* file

commit

```
commit
  [ -f | [ -l | -R ] ]
  [ -F file | -m message ]
  [ -n ]
  [ -r revision ]
  [ files ... ]
```

This command commits the changes made to files in the sandbox to the repository.

The standard meanings of the common client options -l, -n, -r, and -R apply. Additional options are listed in Table 22.

Table 22: commit Options

Option	Description
-f	Force commit, even if no changes are made
-F *file*	Use the contents of the file as the message
-m *message*	Use the message specified

Using the -r option causes the revision to be "sticky," requiring the use of admin -A to continue using the sandbox.

diff

```
diff
  [ -k kflag ]
  [ -l | -R ]
  [ format ]
  [ [ -r rev1 | -D date1 ] [ -r rev2 | -D date2 ] ]
  [ file ... ]
```

The diff command compares two versions of a file and displays the differences in a format determined by the options. By default, the sandbox version of the file is compared to the repository version it was originally copied from.

The standard meanings of the common client options -D, -k, -l, -r, and -R apply.

Table 23 shows some options available with the GNU diff program that are supported by cvs diff. See the GNU diff manual page (man diff) or info page (info diff) for full explanations. If you don't have the GNU version of diff installed, the documentation is available online at *http://www.gnu.org/manual/diffutils-2.7/html_mono/ diff.html* (the GNU web site).

Table 23: diff Format Options

Option	Description
--binary	Treat the files as binary; has no effect on Unix-like systems, but on systems that use a carriage return followed by a line feed as the line-ending sequence, this option causes the carriage return to be treated like any other character, instead of ignoring it as usual
--brief	Tell whether the files differ
-c	Use the context output format
-C nlines --context[=lines]	Show the specified number of lines of context when using context output format

Table 23: diff Format Options (continued)

Option	Description
-t --expand-tabs	Expand tabs to spaces in output
-w --ignore-all-space	Ignore whitespace
-B --ignore-blank-lines	Don't report differences in the number of blank lines
-i --ignore-case	Ignore differences of case
-b --ignore-space-change	Ignore changes in amount of whitespace
-T --initial-tab	Put a tab instead of a space after the indicator character on output, which makes tabs line up correctly in the output
-d --minimal	Use an alternate algorithm that may find smaller diffs, but may take a lot longer to run
-N --new-file	Treat new files as if a zero-length file were present in the other directory (used for making patches)
-n --rcs	Use RCS output format
-s --report-identical-files	Indicate when two files do not differ
-p --show-c-function	For C-like languages, show the names of functions in which differences occur
-y --side-by-side	Show the files side by side

Option	Description
-a --text	Treat files like text, even if they don't seem to be
-u --unified[=*nlines*]	Use the unified diff output format
-U *nlines*	Show this many lines of context on unified diff output format
-V *style*	Control the style of backup files created

edit

```
edit
  [ -a action ]
  [ -l | -R ]
  [ file ... ]
```

The edit command is used in conjunction with the watch command to permit a more coordinated (serialized) development process. It makes the file writeable and sends out an advisory to any users who have requested them. A temporary watch is established and removed automatically when either the unedit or the commit command is issued.

The standard meanings of the common client options -l and -R apply. There is only one additional option that can be used with the edit command, -a *actions*. This option specifies the actions to watch. The legal values for actions are described in the entry for the watch command.

editors

```
editors
  [ -l | -R ]
  [ file ... ]
```

This command displays a list of users working on the files specified. This is determined by checking which users have

---

run the edit command on those files. If the edit command has not been used, no results are displayed.

The standard meanings of the common client options -l and -R apply.

See also the "watch" section.

export

```
export
  [ -d dir [ -N ] ]
  [ -D date | -r rev ]
  [ -f ]
  [ -k kflag ]
  [ -l | -R ]
  [ -n ]
  [ -P ]
  module ...
```

This command exports files from the repository, much like the checkout command, except that the result is not a sandbox (i.e., *CVS* subdirectories are not created). Use this to prepare a directory for distribution. For example:

```
$ cvs export -r foo-1_0 -d foo-1.0 foo
$ tar czf foo-1.0.tar.gz foo-1.0
```

The standard meanings of the common client options -D, -f, -k, -l, -n, -r, and -R apply. Table 24 lists additional options.

Table 24: export Options

Option	Description
-d dir	Use *dir* as the directory name, instead of using the module name
-n	Don't run any checkout programs
-N	Don't shorten paths

When checking out a single file located one or more directories down in a module's directory structure, the -N option can be used with -d to prevent the creation of intermediate directories.

help

```
help
```

This command displays helpful information about the cvs program.

history

```
history
    [ -a | -u user ]
    [ -b string ]
    [ -c ]
    [ -D date ]
    [ -e | -x type ]
    [ -f file | -m module | -n module | -p repository ]...
    [ -l ]
    [ -o ]
    [ -r rev ]
    [ -t tag ]
    [ -T ]
    [ -w ]
    [ -z zone ]
    [ file ... ]
```

This command displays historical information. To use the history command, you must first set up the *history* file in the repository. See the "Repository Structure" section for more information on this file.

When used with the history command, the functions of -f, -l, -n, and -p are not the same as elsewhere in CVS.

The standard meanings of the common client options -D and -r apply. History is reported for activity subsequent to the date or revision indicated. Additional options are listed in Table 25.

Table 25: history Options

Option	Description
-a	Show history for all users (default is current user)
-b *str*	Show history back to the first record containing *str* in the module name, filename, or repository path
-c	Report each commit
-e	Report everything
-f *file*	Show the most recent event for *file*
-l	Show last event only
-m *module*	Produce a full report on *module*
-n *module*	Report the last event for *module*
-o	Report on modules that have been checked out
-p *repository*	Show history for a particular repository directory
-t *tag*	Show history since *tag* was added to the history file
-T	Report on all tags
-u *name*	Show history for a particular user
-w	Show history only for the current working directory
-x *type*	Report on specific types of activity (See Table 26)
-w *zone*	Display times according to the time zone *zone*

The -p option should limit the history report to entries for the directory (or directories, if multiple -p options are specified) given, but as of Version 1.10.8, it doesn't seem to affect the output. For example, to report history for the *CVSROOT* and *hello* modules, run the command:

```
cvs history -p CVSROOT -p hello
```

Using -t is faster than using -r because it searches only the history file, not all of the RCS files.

The record types shown in Table 26 are generated by update commands.

Table 26: Update-Related History Record Types

Type	Description
C	Merge was necessary, but conflicts requiring manual intervention occurred
G	Successful automatic merge
U	Working file copied from repository
W	Working copy deleted

The record types shown in Table 27 are generated by `commit` commands.

Table 27: Commit-Related History Record Types

Type	Description
A	Added for the first time
M	Modified
R	Removed

Each of the record types shown in Table 28 is generated by a different command.

Table 28: Other history Record Types

Type	Command
E	`export`
F	`release`
O	`checkout`
T	`rtag`

Import

```
import
  [ -b branch ]
  [ -d ]
  [ -I pattern ]
  [ -k kflag ]
  [ -m message ]
  [ -W spec ]
  module
```

```
vendor_tag
release_tag ...
```

This command imports an entire directory into the repository as a new module. It incorporates code from outside sources or other code initially created outside the control of the CVS repository. More than one *release_tag* may be specified, in which case multiple symbolic tags are created for the initial revision.

The standard meaning of the common client option -k applies. Additional options are listed in Table 29.

Table 29: import Options

Option	Description
-b *branch*	Import to a vendor branch
-d	Use the modification date and time of the file instead of the current date and time as the import date and time; for local repository locators only
-I *pattern*	Filename patterns for files to ignore
-m *message*	Use *message* as the log message instead of invoking the editor
-W *spec*	Wrapper specification

The -k setting applies only to those files imported during this execution of the command. The keyword substitution modes of files already in the repository are not modified.

When used with -W, the *spec* variable is in the same format as entries in the *cvswrappers* administrative file (see the "The cvswrappers file" section).

Table 30 describes the status codes displayed by the import command.

Table 30: import Status Codes

Status	Description
U	Update; the file is in the repository, and the sandbox version is not different
N	New; the file is new and it has been added to the repository
C	Changed; the file is in the repository, and the sandbox version is different; a merge is required
I	Ignored; the *.cvsignore* file is causing CVS to ignore the file
L	Link; symbolic links are ignored by CVS

log

```
log
  [ -b ]
  [ -d dates ]
  [ -h ]
  [ -N ]
  [ -rrevisions ]
  [ -R ]
  [ -s state ]
  [ -t ]
  [ -wlogins ]
  [ file ... ]
```

This command prints an activity log for the files.

The standard meaning of the common client option -l applies. Additional options are listed in Table 31.

Table 31: log options

Option	Description
-b	List revisions on default branch
-d *dates*	Dates on which to report
-h	Print header only
-N	Don't print tags

Option	Description
-r[*revisions*]	Report on the listed revisions; there is no space between -r and its argument; without an argument, the latest revision of the default branch is used
-R	Print RCS filename only; the usage of -R here is different than elsewhere in CVS (-R usually causes CVS to operate recursively)
-s *state*	Print only those revisions having the specified state
-t	Print only header and descriptive text
-w*logins*	Report on check-ins by the listed logins; there is no space between -w and its argument

For -d, use the date specifications in Table 32. Multiple specifications separated by semicolons may be provided.

Table 32: log Date Range Specifications

Specification	Description
d1<*d2* or *d2*>*d1*	The revisions dated between *d1* and *d2*, exclusive
d1<=*d2* or *d2*>=*d1*	The revisions dated between *d1* and *d2*, inclusive
<*d* or *d*>	The revisions dated before *d*
<=*d* or *d*>=	The revisions dated on or before *d*
d< or >*d*	The revisions dated after *d*
d<= or >=*d*	The revisions dated on or after *d*
d	The most recent revision dated *d* or earlier

For -r, use the revision specifications in Table 33.

Table 33: log Revision Specifications

Specification	Description
rev1: rev2	The revisions between *rev1* and *rev2*, inclusive
:rev	The revisions from the beginning of the branch to *rev*, inclusive
rev:	The revisions from *rev* to the end of the branch, inclusive
branch	All revisions on the branch
branch1: branch2	All revisions on all branches between *branch1* and *branch2*, inclusive
branch.	The latest revision on the branch

For *rev1:rev2*, it is an error if the revisions are not on the same branch.

login

```
login
```

This command logs in to remote repositories. The password entered is cached in the ˜/.cvspass file, since a connection to the server is not maintained across invocations.

logout

```
logout
```

This command logs out of a remote repository. The password cached in the ˜/.cvspass file is deleted.

rdiff

```
rdiff
  [ -c | -s | -u ]
  [ { { -D date1 | -r rev1 } [ -D date2 | -r rev2 ] } | -t ]
  [ -f ]
  [ -l | -R ]
  [-V vn]
  file ...
```

The rdiff command creates a patch file that can convert a directory containing one release to a different release.

The standard meanings of the common client options -D, -f, -l, -r, and -R apply. Additional options are listed in Table 34.

Table 34: rdiff Options

Option	Description
-c	Use context diff format (the default)
-s	Output a summary of changed files instead of a patch file
-t	Show the differences between the two most recent revisions
-u	Use unified diff format[a]
-V rcsver	Obsolete; used to specify version of RCS to emulate for keyword expansion (keyword expansion emulates RCS Version 5)

[a] Not all versions of diff and patch support the unified diff format, so use -u with caution.

release

```
release
  [ -d ]
  directory ...
```

Sandboxes can be abandoned or deleted without using cvs release if desired; using the release command logs an entry to the *history* file (if this mechanism is configured) about the sandbox being destroyed. In addition, it checks the disposition (recursively) of each of the sandbox files before deleting anything. This helps prevent destroying work that has not yet been committed.

There is only one option that is used with the release command, -d. The -d option deletes the sandbox copy if no uncommitted changes are present.

New directories (and the files they contain) in the sandbox are deleted if the -d option is used with the release command.

The status codes listed in Table 35 describe the disposition of each file encountered in the repository and the sandbox.

Table 35: release Status Codes

Status	Description
A	The sandbox file has been added (the file was created and cvs add was run), but the addition has not been committed.
M	The sandbox copy of the file has been modified.
P U	Update available. There is a newer version of the file in the repository, and the copy in the sandbox has not been modified.
R	The sandbox copy was removed (the file was deleted and cvs remove was run), but the removal was not committed.
?	The file is present in the sandbox, but not in the repository.

remove

```
remove
  [ -f ]
  [ -l | -R ]
  [ file ... ]
```

Indicate that files should be removed from the repository. The files aren't removed until they are committed. Use cvs add to resurrect files that have been removed if you change your mind later.

The standard meanings of the common client options -l and -R apply. Only one other option is used with the remove command, -f. When used, -f deletes the file from the sandbox first.

rtag

```
rtag
  [ -a ]
  [ -b ]
  [ -d ]
  [ -D date | -r rev ]
  [ -f ]
```

```
[ -F ]
[ -l | - R ]
[ -n ]
tag
file ...
```

Assign a tag to a particular revision of a set of files. If the file already uses the tag for a different revision, cvs rtag complains unless the -F option is used. This command does not refer to the sandbox file revisions (use cvs tag for that), so it can be run outside a sandbox if desired.

The standard meanings of the common client options -D, -f, -l, -r, and -R apply. Additional options are listed in Table 36.

Table 36: rtag Options

Option	Description
-a	Search the *Attic* for removed files containing the tag
-b	Make a branch tag
-d	Delete the tag
-F	Force; move the tag from its current revision to the one specified
-n	Don't run any tag program from the *modules* file

status

```
status
  [ -l | -R ]
  [ -v ]
  [ file ... ]
```

Display the status of the files.

The standard meanings of the common client options -l and -R apply. The other option used with the status command, -v, can include tag information.

tag

```
tag
  [ -b ]
  [ -c ]
  [ -d ]
  [ -D date | -r rev ]
  [ -f ]
  [ -F ]
  [ -l | R ]
  tag
  [ file ... ]
```

Assign a tag to the sandbox revisions of a set of files. You can use the status -v command to list the existing tags for a file.

The *tag* must start with a letter and consist entirely of letters, numbers, dashes (-), and underscores (_). Therefore, while you might want to tag your *hello* project with 1.0 when you release Version 1.0, you must tag it with something like hello-1_0 instead.

The standard meanings of the common client options -D, -f, -l, -r, and -R apply. Additional options are listed in Table 37.

Table 37: tag Options

Option	Description
-b	Make a branch tag
-c	Check for changes; make sure the files are not locally modified before tagging
-d	Delete the tag
-F	Force; move the tag from its current revision to the one specified

Since the -d option destroys information that might be important, it is recommended that you use it only when absolutely necessary. It is usually better to create a different tag with a similar name.

unedit

```
unedit
  [ -l | -R ]
  [ file ... ]
```

Abandon file modifications and make the file read-only again.
Watchers are notified.

The standard meanings of the common client options -l and
-R apply.

update

```
update
  [ -A ]
  [ -d ]
  [ -D date | -r rev ]
  [ -f ]
  [ -I pattern ]
  [ -j rev1 [ -j rev2 ] ]
  [ -k kflag ]
  [ -l | -R ]
  [ -p ]
  [ -P ]
  [ -W spec ]
  [ file ... ]
```

Update the sandbox, merging in any changes from the repository. For example:

```
cvs -n -q update -AdP
```

can be used to do a quick status check of the current sandbox
versus the head of the revision of the trunk branch.

The standard meanings of the common client options -D, -f,
-k, -l, -r, and -R apply. Additional options are listed in Table
38.

Option	Description
-A	Reset sticky tags
-d	Create and update new directories
-I *pattern*	Filename patterns for files to ignore
-j *revision*	Merge in (or "join") changes between two revisions
-p	Check out files to standard output
-P	Prune empty directories
-W *spec*	Wrapper specification

Using -D or -r results in sticky dates or tags, respectively, on the affected files (using -p along with these prevents stickiness). Use -A to reset any sticky tags or dates.

If two -j specifications are made, the differences between them are computed and applied to the current file. If only one is given, the common ancestor of the sandbox revision and the specified revision are used as a basis for computing differences to be merged.

For example, suppose a project has an experimental branch, and important changes to the file *foo.c* are introduced between revisions 1.2.2.1 and 1.2.2.2. Once those changes prove stable, you want them reflected in the main line of development. From a sandbox with the head revisions checked out, run:

```
$ cvs update -j 1.2.2.1 -j 1.2.2.2 foo.c
```

CVS finds the differences between the two revisions and applies those differences to the file in the sandbox.

The *spec* used with -W is in the same format as entries in the *cvswrappers* administrative file (see the "The cvswrappers file" section).

The status codes listed in Table 39 describe the action taken on each file encountered in the repository and the sandbox.

Table 39: update Status Codes

Status Code	Description
A	Added. Server took no action because there was no repository file. Indicates that cvs add has been run, but not cvs commit.
C	Conflict. Sandbox copy is modified (it has been edited since it was checked out or last committed). There was a new revision in the repository and there were conflicts when CVS merged its changes into the sandbox version.
M	Modified. Sandbox copy is modified (it has been edited since it was checked out or last committed). If there was a new revision in the repository, its changes were successfully merged into the file (no conflicts).
P	Patched. Same as U (updated), but indicates the server used a patch.
R	Removed. Server took no action. Indicates that cvs remove has been run, but not cvs commit.
U	Updated. The file was brought up to date.
?	File is present in sandbox, but not in repository.

watch

```
watch
  { { on | off } | { add | remove } [ -a action ] }
  [ -l | -R ]
  file ...
```

The watch command controls CVS's edit-tracking mechanism. By default, CVS operates in its concurrent development mode, allowing any user to edit any file at any time. CVS includes this watch mechanism to support developers who would rather be notified of edits made by others proactively rather than discover them when doing an update.

The *CVSROOT/notify* file determines how notifications are performed.

Table 40 shows the watch subcommands and their uses.

Table 40: watch Subcommands

Subcommand	Description
add	Start watching files
off	Turn off watching
on	Turn on watching
remove	Stop watching files

The standard meanings of the common client options -l and -R apply. The only other option that can be used with the watch command is -a *action*. The -a option is used with one of the actions listed in Table 41.

Table 41: watch Actions

Action	Description
all	All of the items below in this table
commit	A user has committed changes
edit	A user ran cvs edit
none	Don't watch; used by the edit command
unedit	A user ran cvs unedit, cvs release, or deleted the file and ran cvs update, recreating it

See also the descriptions of the edit, editors, unedit, and watchers commands.

watchers

```
watchers
  [ -l | -R ]
  [ file ... ]
```

This command displays a list of users watching the specified files. This is determined by checking which users have run the watch command on a particular file (or set of files). If the watch command has not been used, no results are displayed.

The standard meanings of the common client options -l and -R apply. See also the "watch" section.

CVS Utilities

There are many CVS-related programs freely available on the Internet. This section references a few of them.

Emacs CVS Mode

GNU Emacs (*http://www.gnu.org/software/emacs/emacs.html*) has a built-in mode (called VC Mode) for working with CVS. See *GNU Emacs Pocket Reference* by Debra Cameron (O'Reilly & Associates) for more information.

Perl

The following Perl modules can be used to build solutions around CVS:

cvs2cl.pl
> (*http://www.red-bean.com/~kfogel/cvs2cl.shtml*) By Karl Fogel. Converts CVS log messages to GNU-style ChangeLog entries.

takepatch.pl
> (*http://www.loth.demon.co.uk/takepatch.pl*) By Steve Dodd. Applies a unified patch file to a CVS working directory, adding new files and directories, and removing old files if necessary.

CVS Clients

The CVS distribution includes a complete command-line client implementation. In addition, there are many graphical client programs for accessing CVS repositories:

Cervisia
> (*http://cervisia.sourceforge.net*) A CVS frontend for *KDE* (*http://www.kde.org*).

LinCVS

    (*http://ppprs1.phy.tu-dresden.de/~trogisch/linux/lincvsen.html*)
A graphical Linux CVS client written with the Qt toolkit
(*http://www.trolltech.com/products/qt.html*).

pcl-cvs

    (*ftp://rum.cs.yale.edu/pub/monnier/pcl-cvs*)   By   Stefan
Monnier. An Emacs `dired`-like CVS mode.

Pharmacy

    (*http://home.earthlink.net/~nawalker/pharmacy*)   A   CVS
frontend for *GNOME* (*http://www.gnome.org*).

WinCvs

    (*http://www.wincvs.org*)   A   CVS   client   for   Microsoft
Windows.

CVS Web Interfaces

These CVS client interfaces allow you to view the contents of
a repository with a web browser:

cvsweb

    By Bill Fenner, Henner Zeller, et al. (*http://lem-
ming.stud.fh-heilbronn.de/~zeller/cgi/cvsweb.cgi*). A Perl-
and CGI-based web interface to CVS repositories.

ViewCVS

    By Greg Stein (*http://www.lyra.org/greg/python/viewcvs*).
A Python- and CGI-based web interface to CVS
repositories.

Index

More Titles from O'Reilly

Linux

Using Samba

By Peter Kelly, Perry Donham &
David Collier-Brown
1st Edition November 1999
416 pages, Includes CD-ROM
ISBN 1-56592-449-5

Linux Network Administrator's Guide, 2nd Edition

By Olaf Kirch & Terry Dawson
2nd Edition June 2000
506 pages, ISBN 1-56592-400-2

Linux Device Drivers

By Alessandro Rubini
1st Edition February 1998
442 pages, ISBN 1-56592-292-1

Programming with GNU Software

By Mike Loukides & Andy Oram
1st Edition December 1996
260 pages, Includes CD-ROM
ISBN 1-56592-112-7

Building Linux Clusters

By David HM Spector
1st Edition July 2000
352 pages, Includes CD-ROM
ISBN 1-56592-625-0

UNIX Power Tools, 2nd Edition

By Jerry Peek, Tim O'Reilly & Mike Loukides
2nd Edition August 1997
1120 pages, Includes CD-ROM
ISBN 1-56592-260-3

Understanding the Linux Kernel

By Daniel P. Bovet & Marco Cesati
1st Edition October 2000
650 pages, ISBN 0-596-00002-2

MySQL & mSQL

By Randy Jay Yarger, George Reese & Tim King
1st Edition July 1999
506 pages, ISBN 1-56592-434-7

Linux

Linux in a Nutshell, 3rd Edition

*By Ellen Siever, Stephen Spainhour,
Jessica P. Hekman, & Stephen Figgins*
3rd Edition August 2000
800 pages, ISBN 0-596-00025-1

Evil Geniuses in a Nutshell

By Illiad
1st Edition April 2000
132 pages, ISBN 1-56592-861-X

Learning Debian GNU/Linux

By Bill McCarty
1st Edition September 1999
360 pages, Includes CD-ROM
ISBN 1-56592-705-2

Running Linux, 3rd Edition

*By Matt Welsh, Matthias Kalle Dalheimer &
Lar Kaufman*
3rd Edition August 1999
752 pages, ISBN 1-56592-469-X

GIMP Pocket Reference

By Sven Neumann
1st Edition October 2000
112 pages, ISBN 1-56592-731-1

Learning the bash Shell, 2nd Edition

By Cameron Newham & Bill Rosenblatt
2nd Edition January 1998
336 pages, ISBN 1-56592-347-2

Photoshop 6 Cookbook

By Donnie O'Quinn
1st Edition February 2001 (est.)
504 pages (est.), ISBN 1-56592-669-2

The Cathedral & the Bazaar

By Eric S. Raymond
1st Edition October 1999
288 pages, ISBN 1-56592-724-9